LIVE ACTION ENGLISH
For Foreign Students
(Læffs)

by Elizabeth Romijn & Contee Seely

Foreword by James J. Asher

illustrated by Elizabeth Romijn

Student Text   Eighth Edition

The Alemany Press
P.O. Box 5265
San Francisco, Ca. 94101

OTHER BOOKS BY CONTEE SEELY

- ¡ESPAÑOL CON IMPACTO!
- HOW TO USE TPR

First edition: April, 1979
Second edition: August, 1979
Third edition: April, 1980
Fourth edition: December, 1980
Fifth edition: August, 1981
Sixth edition: April, 1982
Seventh edition: November, 1982
Eighth edition: December, 1983

Copyright © 1979 by Elizabeth Romijn and Contee Seely. All rights reserved. No part of this book may be reproduced or transmitted in any form or by any means, electronic or mechanical, including photocopying, recording, or by any information storage and retrieval system, without permission in writing from the authors.

Printed in the U.S.A.

ISBN 0-88084-025-0

CONTENTS

For the Teacher:
Foreword iv
Introduction v
Notes to the Fifth Edition vii
General Procedures for Enacting Each Series viii
Creative Adaptations xiv

Washing Your Hands	1	A Magic Trick	37
Candle	2	Writing a Letter	38
Getting Home	3	Going to the Movies	39
Cheese	4	Making a Grocery List	40
Balloon	5	Grocery Shopping	41
Chewing Gum	6	Fight	42
A Hiding Game	7	Haircut	43
Vitamin Pill	8	Eating Oranges	44
Sharpening Your Pencil	9	Rainy Day	45
Breakfast Cereal	10	A Rough Bus Ride	46
Shopping for a Coat	11	Building a Fire	47
A Glass of Milk	12	Going Swimming	48
Wrapping a Present	13	A Piece of Toast	49
Good Morning	14	A Bird	50
You're Getting Sick	15	A Beautiful Day	51
Office Worker	16	A Party!	52
Sewing On a Button	17	Time to Clean House	53
Painting a Picture	18	Car Ride	54
Taking the Plane	19	Dog	55
Stop! Thief!	20	A Man Getting Ready to Go Out	56
Restaurant	21	A Woman Getting Ready for a Date	57
Opening a Present	22		
A Balloon Trick	23		
Ice Cream and T.V.	24	At the Laundromat	58
Taking Care of a Baby	25	Doctor's Appointment	59
A Broken Glass	26	Putting Drops in Your Eyes	60
To the Moon and Back	27	Putting Up a Towel Rack	61
Let's Play Ball	28	Cashier	62
Hungry Bugs	29	Taking Pictures	63
Using a Pay Phone	30	Making a Table	64
Soup for Lunch	31	A Jack-O-Lantern for Halloween	65
Changing a Light Bulb	32		
Bloody Knee	33	A Thanksgiving Feast	66
Scrambled Eggs	34	Check, Credit Card and Driver's License	67
Bank	35		
A Broken Plate	36		

FOREWORD

In 20 years of research we have found that when students respond with appropriate actions to commands, their learning is far more efficient and their involvement fuller than if they do not move. In English, for example, it is not enough for students to understand the meaning of *stand up* and *sit down*. They must construct their own reality by physically standing when they hear "stand up" and sitting when they hear "sit down." The lessons in this book are based, first and foremost, on this principle (Secondarily they are based on Gouin's discovery that series help the memory.).

The authors do not assume that the students who use this book know no English. Nor do they assume that the instructor will do nothing more than use the material here presented. With students who are beginning at the lowest levels, we have discovered that an optimal format is for them to start by silently listening to directions in the target language and responding with appropriate actions. Speaking from students is delayed until comprehension has been thoroughly internalized. Eventually, as comprehension of the target language expands and expands, talk will spontaneously appear. Of course, like infants learning their first language, when speech appears, there will be many distortions. But gradually, in time, with the skillful coaching of the instructor, student speech will shape itself in the direction of the native speaker. The procedures recommended in this book are one well-developed way to provide this coaching and will also help students who have not had the good fortune to begin their language learning with this exciting approach.

The publication of this book is especially welcome, as it is the first student text that makes use of Total Physical Response to be published in the English-speaking world.

James J. Asher

INTRODUCTION

This book consists of 66 series of commands which are actually put into action by every member of a class, thereby creating live situations. It is not a complete course. However, it will combine unusually well with all sorts of other materials at the beginning and intermediate levels. It is unusually well-suited to the multi-level class, because students at both levels—and often advanced students too—learn with full involvement in every series. It is also extremely good for open-enrollment classes, because reviewing is just as lively as enacting the material for the first time.

Very few groups or teachers are accustomed to working in the manner in which these series are most profitably used. So, although the lessons may be used in any order, we recommend that you start with some of the simpler, briefer, more obvious ones. The first 18 lessons are especially appropriate for this purpose.

Some teachers who are new to this approach will find certain things about the classroom procedures unusual and a little uncomfortable at first. During the presentation (step 2, "Procedures," p. x) the students remain silent while listening and watching the action. This silence can seem strange but is necessary for good hearing and comprehension and subsequent pronunciation. In the final step (#7, p. xii) all the students practice in a tremendous babble that often appears chaotic but is actually very efficient, allowing each student far more opportunity for real communication than in the usual language class. Another unusual aspect is the emotional expression, exaggerated action and theatrical drama required of the instructor.

These series have been used successfully with Latin-Americans, Chinese, Koreans, Vietnamese, East Indians, Japanese, Thais, Laotians, Cambodians, Filipinos, Samoans, Swedes, Russians, Italians and French—all of whom have responded enthusiastically.

The approach on which this book is based has its roots in the work of Frenchman François Gouin, Englishman Harold E. Palmer and American James J. Asher. Gouin published *L'art d'enseigner et d'étudier les langues* in 1880 (Paris: Librairie Fischbacher) (English translation by H. Swan & V. Bétis, *The Art of Teaching and Studying Languages*. London: Philip,

v

1892.). He gave a detailed description of the use of series without making mention of enacting them. In Palmer's *English through Actions* (co-authored by his daughter, Dorothée Palmer, Tokyo: Institute of Research in Language Teaching, 1925. Slightly revised later edition: London: Longman, 1959.) debt was paid to Gouin and action was brought into prominence. Asher (who wrote the foreword to this book) has done 20 years of research which has clearly established the high effectiveness of "Total Physical Response" with students of all ages. A psychologist at San José State University, he has published numerous articles describing his research and a book entitled *Learning Another Language Through Actions: The Complete Teacher's Guidebook* (Sky Oaks Productions, 19544 Sky Oaks Way, Los Gatos, California 95030; 1977), as well as producing several films which demonstrate this approach.

We wish to thank Maggie Seely, Jaap Romijn, Eduardo Hernández Chávez, Ken Beck, Judy Winn-Bell Olsen, Helen Valdez, Helen McCully, Patricia Helton and James Asher for their constant encouragement. Our greatest thanks go to our students who have been our inspiration over the last 4½ years. These materials have grown and developed in direct response to their joy and enthusiasm in learning this way. We wish you and your students the same enthusiasm and joy.

Please Note

You are welcome to observe the authors using these materials in their language classes in the San Francisco Bay Area. Elizabeth (Libby) Romijn teaches ESL for the Mission Community College Center in San Francisco, usually in the mornings. Call (415) 863-3887 for location. Contee Seely teaches ESL for the Neighborhood Centers' Adult Education Program in the Oakland public schools, usually in the afternoons—call (415) 452-1405—and Spanish at his Command Performance Language School, usually in the evenings. Call (415) 526-2583 for information.

NOTES TO THE FIFTH EDITION

RECEPTIVE and EXPRESSIVE STAGES and READING and WRITING

The first three steps in the procedures are the listening or receptive stage. Step #4 is reading and possibly writing. Students generally should not proceed to reading or writing until they are ready for the speaking or expressive stage, which is steps 5 to 7. The key to readiness to proceed is *unhesitating facility in responding to the commands*. If your students are children at or below puberty, they would normally not copy the series until they have completed *all* other steps.

USING THIS BOOK WITH VERY LOW BEGINNERS

With very new learners of English, we suggest you *not* begin by using the full procedures given on pages *viii* to *xiii*. By "very low beginners" we mean learners who are *really new* to English, who have virtually no experience of any kind with English. Some such learners may have no familiarity with the Latin alphabet or any system of writing.

Such learners need to hear and experience English in a meaningful context for a considerable period of time before they are encouraged to speak it at all.

Here are some ways to ease new learners into English:

1. Do only the first three steps of the procedures, going over numerous series several times each before you ever encourage the learners to say anything in any series. This way they will internalize the material *very thoroughly* before speaking it and will be very comfortable with it when they finally do say it.

2. Simplify the series considerably. See #2 in "Creative Adaptations" on page *xiv*.

3. Choose some of the simpler commands from various series and work on these for some time with students listening and responding physically. You can use recombinations by using different nouns with whatever verbs you choose, as in #5 on page *xv*.

4. Devise and do *very* brief action dialogs. See page *xvii*, #10. Be sure every student is adequately prepared before s/he does a dialog on her/his own. This means s/he (a) has experienced it before her/his eyes in a meaningful context many times and (b) has heard good, natural (but *not* fast) pronunciation several times for imitation and has heard it very well.

GENERAL PROCEDURES FOR ENACTING EACH SERIES

The final objective of these procedures is for each student to be able to tell another student to perform the series at hand and, conversely, to be able to respond physically to another person's delivery of the commands. The first six of the following steps are used as a method of preparing students to be ready to work effectively and independently in the seventh and final step:

1. Setting up (1-2 minutes)

2. Initial demonstration of series (1-2 minutes)

3. Group live action (2-3 minutes)

4. Written copy (2-10 minutes, depending on whether or not students must copy it from the board)

5. Oral repetition and question/answer period (5-10 minutes)

6. Student(s) producing/other person responding (5-10 minutes)

7. Students all working in pairs (5-15 minutes)

The first six steps are only suggestions and can be changed or alternated. Experiment and do whatever you find necessary to properly prepare students for #7.

If you ever run out of time during a class session, start at the beginning again at the next session. The review will go faster and make things easier for everybody.

A detailed description of each of the suggested procedures follows.

BEFOREHAND—PREPARING REALIA

These lessons are specifically intended to be used with props. If you have never used props before, you may question the validity of spending the time to gather and prepare them. We have found that they are invaluable not only as a source of fun but as an aid to comprehension and retention. The less sophisticated the students, the more realistic and obvious the presentation needs to be, so that the language will truly be about a "happening" which is affecting their muscles and their senses. Totally experiencing the situation makes a strong impression and connects the words to something real, making learning much easier, more effective and more enjoyable for any student.

1. SETTING UP and Working Into the Series

    Set up your situation in front of the students' eyes—as they are assembling at the beginning of class, or as they are finishing up some other work, or even with their full attention. For some series this will only involve laying out some props. Sometimes you can improvise with whatever is available. For example, in "Bank" (p. 35) the rungs in the back of a chair or a Venetian blind may serve as the teller's window. Or an aisle can be a city street or a diving board. In other series you may need an illustration of a certain room or scene (commercially produced, cut from a magazine, or simply drawn by a student or yourself on the board), such as the downtown street in "Shopping for a New Coat" (p. 11), the phone booth in "Pay Phone" (p. 30) or the fireplace in "Building a Fire" (p. 47). In still others, such as "Doctor's Appointment" (p. 59) and "Haircut" (p. 43), you'll need to recruit some students for minor roles and introduce them as the receptionist, the nurse, the doctor, the barber, etc.

    Talk about what you are doing in order to work into the series naturally and casually. For example, for "Washing Your Hands" (p. 1) you might make remarks such as, "Now I'm going to wash my hands" or "Oh, look at this; my hands are dirty" (maybe they really are, from something else you've been doing). Then, as you set out each object, ask if anyone knows its name. Hold up the soap and ask, "What do you call this?" and repeat with the towel and the faucet. If anyone would understand the words "sink" and "bathroom," indicate that you are in the bathroom or at the sink. If your class is small, you may even go to a real sink for the initial demonstration.

2. INITIAL DEMONSTRATION OF SERIES

Now ask the class not to talk any more: "Don't talk; don't repeat; only look and listen." *It is essential that everyone be paying attention to the action now.*

If you have a student who might understand some or all of the commands in the series, or an aide or a visitor, have that person respond physically to your reading (with *loads* of expression!) of the series. If no such person is available, demonstrate the action yourself the first time. Take plenty of time to make sure each action is fully understood. If you're not sure that everyone followed it, repeat it once or twice, using the same "performer" again, or a new one each time. You or the performer(s) may have to use pantomime for some actions.

3. GROUP LIVE ACTION

Thank your performer and address the entire class with, "Now *you're* going to wash *your* hands." You might even begin with, "Look at *your* hands! They're dirty! Ugh! Turn on the water, etc."

You will probably have to ask again that no one repeat or talk at all during this time. Now they are to respond physically to the imperatives, experiencing the words as real communication, learning with their muscles, *living* the language. Usually not every person has every object in the series. So they can pantomime the actions which they cannot actually perform. Many people need some prodding at this point. If someone does not turn the water on, you might hand that person the faucet and repeat, "Please turn on the water." If some people don't wash their hands, you might ask, "Where's your soap?" If some people say they don't need to do these things because they already understand them, tell them that although understanding is of course necessary, it's not enough, that they will *remember* the words much better if they *experience* them.

Some adults may even be a little insulted at first, feeling that these little pantomimes are childish. However, we have never seen any students continue to feel this way after one lesson, because they realize very quickly how much they are learning and how easily. Even advanced students learn some new words and usages in most series.

Note especially: It is advisable to go through step 3 several times on different occasions (thereby allowing students to thoroughly internalize the series) before they read it and produce it orally. The lower the level of the class, the more times it is necessary to do this.

4. WRITTEN COPY

   When all the students can respond physically to the series, have them finally look at it. If copies of the book are not available, simply write the series clearly on the chalkboard for the students to copy themselves. Copying it is a useful exercise in itself, especially for students with little education. It is also handy, for step #5, to have this large copy on the board so that you can point out individual words and phrases.

5. ORAL REPETITION and QUESTION/ANSWER PERIOD

   When everyone has a copy, have the students repeat each line after you, taking plenty of time to go over individual words which are particularly difficult to pronounce or understand. *Make sure every student can hear your pronunciation fully.* If s/he can't, s/he won't be able to pronounce well. Try to answer questions about meaning with motions rather than translations.

   Some students panic at the sight of written words, especially in English, and fail to realize that these are the same words that they have just understood aurally and have responded to appropriately. This would need to be brought to their attention, even if it means your going through the actions again each time you read or point to a line.

   Give the students some extra time to look over the series and ask more questions. This might also be a good time to point out some minimal pairs—soap/soup, wash/watch—and do some work on these.

6. STUDENT(S) PRODUCING/OTHER PERSON RESPONDING

   Now ask for a volunteer, or choose a student, to tell *you* to do the entire series. Or, since each line is numbered, assign several individuals a line or two by number. If you only take volunteers at this point, probably some students will never read, so it is best to *choose* readers, at least sometimes.

This is a good opportunity for you to hear pronunciation problems. Generally, if one student has a problem pronouncing a certain word or phrase, there are others too, and this means more group practice is needed. Make sure the students hear well. This is the first essential for good pronunciation.

Next you may want to have one student do the physical responses in front of the class or at his or her desk as another student reads. There may be a new student or less responsive student who doesn't seem to be following the language. This is a good time to find out if this is just shyness, or confusion about the new method, or if indeed s/he doesn't understand what is being said. Whatever the problem is, it can probably be ironed out as that student follows the other's commands, with some encouraging prompting from you.

You may want to have more students tell you or the whole class to do the series. Remember that what you're doing is preparing them to do the series unsupervised. Whether or not you go on or repeat steps 5 and/or 6 a few times depends on how the students are sounding and responding.

7. STUDENTS ALL WORKING IN PAIRS

When you feel that the students are clear enough on the language of the series (comprehending, responding, pronouncing), ask them to work in pairs or threes, one telling (or reading) and the other(s) listening and responding physically. In doing so, each student will experience the power of actually speaking English and having his or her commands acted upon by another person, thus truly communicating in English about something which is actually occurring.

You may form the groups yourself to allow greater learning opportunities, or you may let the class form its own pairs or threes. Make sure everyone has a partner (or partners).

This also frees the instructor to work individually with students. You can evaluate the lesson, your presentation of it, the students' grasp of it and individual progress. Your job now changes from director to aide. Go around the room listening, helping, correcting, approving, encouraging reluctant students to practice ("for your memory"). Make sure every student goes through the series at least twice—once telling, once responding. More advanced students, or those who have done this series before, can be encouraged to try it without looking at the copy. Answer questions people may have been too shy to ask before the group.

It is helpful to get a student who is used to working this way to break in a new student. However, occasionally new students may need to have *you* work individually with them, physically going through the entire series, as an example of the way you mean for them to work.

Usually some students will need more guidance than others on how to use this time. People who spend the whole time recopying the lesson or looking up and translating words may be doing so simply because they don't know what else to do. Point out that these are things that can be done at home, and that this time is basically for oral practice and realistic response.

However, do let the students follow their own impulses. You will be surprised at the large variety of things different people will work on at this time. The more freedom you give them, the more that will happen. Furthermore, some of the activities that may seem irrelevant or even counterproductive to you, may in fact be serving some important purpose for the students involved. Even simply recopying may be as important as anything else to a student illiterate in his or her native language and as much as s/he can handle on a particular occasion. Different people have different ways of learning, of fixing things in their minds, and of checking out their own comprehension and mastery of what has just transpired. Give them plenty of time to tie up the loose ends as they see them. And keep your eyes and ears open. Your sensitivity to the situation can help some individuals immensely and can help you know how to deal better with other series.

You may review a series at any time. Generally you will find retention notably better than with other types of exercises. And the review will improve it even more.

These procedures are useful, with minor adaptations, to prepare students to do other kinds of work in pairs, as well as series. Many teachers have been unsuccessful in their previous attempts at having students work in pairs. The main source of difficulty is that the students have not been adequately prepared. Using the above procedures, students *are* properly prepared.

CREATIVE ADAPTATIONS

To a much greater degree than most material, these lessons offer taking-off points for creative use of the vocabulary they contain. Some examples:

1. Verb-form practice in present, past and future. For instance, "A Glass of Milk" (p. 12) would go like this in the past: First the teacher or a student does all the actions in silence or in response to someone's commands, while the (other)students watch. Then the person who has done the actions says, "I poured myself a glass of milk. I spilled some of it on the table...." Then all the students repeat the words after the teacher, with emphasis on the past forms. And finally all the students go through this in pairs or threes, one person at a time acting, then speaking to the other(s). In present continuous you say, "I'm pouring myself a glass of milk..." and in *"going to* future," "I'm going to pour myself a glass of milk." In all cases the actions are done at the appropriate time in relation to the words spoken. Time expressions may be taught and included: *first, then, after that, finally, now, right now* ... Virtually the same process may be used in different persons—*you, he, she, we, you* (plural), *they*—with the proper persons performing. For all of these except *you* (singular) and *we*, groups of 3 or 4 are needed.

2. For raw beginners, some of the series can be shortened. For example, "Changing a Light Bulb" (p. 32) may become:

   1. Turn on the light. It's burned out!
   2. Go get a new one.
   3. Unscrew the old bulb.
   4. Screw the new one in.
   5. Turn it on. It works!

3. The teacher asks the students questions which are about themselves or otherwise of interest, using the vocabulary of the lesson in whatever tense(s) desired.

4. Students ask questions of the teacher and of other students. Sometimes you may wish to ask them to practice a particular tense.

5. Use the same commands but with different contexts, different objects. For instance, using "Getting Home" (p. 3) as your take-off point, tell people to:

> Go downtown. (Use a picture.)
>
> Walk (or go) downstairs.
>
> Take out your pencil.
>
> Put it in your pocket.
>
> Unlock the window.
>
> Put your pen away.
>
> Turn the knob on the T.V.
>
> Open your mouth.
>
> Close it.
>
> Lock the car. (Use picture.)
>
> Turn on the radio.

Then get the students to tell you and other students to do different things, using the same verbs. It is often useful to write the verbs with some possible nouns to combine them with on the blackboard to stimulate creative use by students and to get them to lift their heads. You can use all the verbs in the series in your list or just select certain ones. Five to ten is a good working set. For example:

go (to)	door
walk (to)	padlock
unlock	outside
turn	cupboard
lock	
close	downstairs
open	

and so on.

Sentences created may be, for instance, "Unlock the cupboard," "Open the cupboard," "Walk outside".... Students may help you choose nouns for the list and may of course use other nouns while practicing.

6. Along the same lines as #5 above, improvise entire new situations, using much vocabulary from series already enacted. As you do this, some new vocabulary often emerges. As long as the meaning of it is demonstrable, this will cause no problem. In fact, some people will pick some of it up right away. The scenario that develops may be very ordinary and calm or extravagant and wild. You may do the usual kind of work with any of these improvised series or you can drop them and go on to other things. Students may also improvise their own series. Or they may write them down for subsequent use (perhaps after correction). You may too.

7. Students (and teacher) can write mini-plays for performance, involving other material as well as commands. After a number of series have been enacted by students, they will be accumstomed to using English with live action, and mini-plays come easier than otherwise would be the case.

8. The non-verb vocabulary of a series may also be focused on with commands. For example, from "Scrambled Eggs" (p. 34) you or your students can produce:

> Throw me an *egg*.
>
> Put the *egg beater* away.
>
> Pass the *salt* please.
>
> Pour *a little milk* in the *pan*.
>
> Go get a *dry* towel.

9. You may write your own series to suit the particular needs or environment of your students. Vocational ESL classes, for instance, have specialized vocabulary which could be taught most effectively using this approach.

10. Very brief dialogs (2-6 lines) may be written and enacted after adequate preparation (see "General Procedures"). For example:

> 1 — Will you scratch my back?
>
> 2 — Sure, but *first* you scratch *my* back.
>
> *Then* I'll scratch *your* back.
>
> 1 — O.K.

Try this one and you'll see how much fun these little dialogs can be.

WASHING YOUR HANDS

1. You're going to wash your hands.

2. Turn on the water.

3. Pick up the soap.

4. Wash your hands.

5. Put the soap down.

6. Rinse your hands.

7. Turn off the water.

8. Pick up the towel.

9. Dry your hands.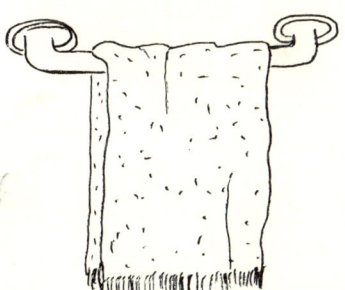

10. Put the towel on the towel rack.

CANDLE

1. Put the candle in the candle holder.

2. Take out your matches.

3. Tear out a match.

4. Light the match.

5. Light the candle.

6. Blow out the match.

7. Throw it away.

8. Put the matches away.

9. Look at the candle.

10. Smell it.

11. Blow it out.

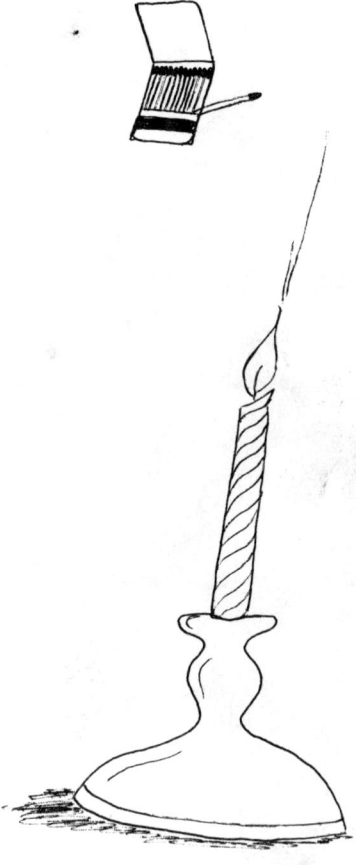

GETTING HOME

1. Go home.

2. Walk upstairs.

3. Take out your key.

4. Put it in the keyhole.

5. Unlock the door.

6. Put the key away.

7. Turn the doorknob.

8. Open the door.

9. Go in.

10. Close the door.

11. Lock it.

12. Turn on the light.

13. Sit down and rest.

CHEESE

1. Unwrap the cheese.

2. ~~Put it on the cutting board.~~

3. Pick up the knife.

4. Cut a little piece of cheese.

5. Try it.

6. Cut another piece.

7. Eat it.

8. Cut a big piece.

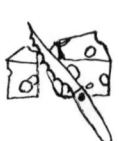

9. Take a bite.

10. Chew it up and swallow it.

11. Take another bite.

12. Eat it all.

13. Wrap up the rest of the cheese.

BALLOON

1. You're going to play with a balloon.

2. Stretch the balloon.

3. Stretch it more.

4. Let go of one end.

5. Blow up the balloon.

6. Don't tie it.

7. Let the air out slowly.

8. Watch the balloon shrink.

9. Blow it up again.

10. Squeeze it but don't pop it.

11. Let go of it and watch it fly.

CHEWING GUM

1. Go to the store.

2. Buy a pack of gum.

3. Open the pack.

4. Take out a piece of gum.

5. Unwrap it.

6. Put it in your mouth.

7. Chew it.

8. Don't swallow it.

9. Take the wrapper to the waste basket.

10. Throw it away.

11. Put the pack of gum away.

A HIDING GAME

1. We're going to play a game.

2. Mary, close your eyes.

3. Don't open them.

4. John, hide the _____.

5. Mary, open your eyes.

6. Get up.

7. Look for the _____.

    Colder.   Warmer!   HOT!

8. (Mary says:) "Oh, here it is!"

9. Good! You found it!

VITAMIN PILL

1. You're going to take your vitamins.

2. Pick up the bottle of vitamin pills.

3. Take the top off.

4. Take out a pill.

5. Put the top back on.

6. Put the bottle down.

7. Put the pill in your mouth.

8. Drink some water and swallow the pill.

9. Uh-oh! It's stuck in your throat!

10. Drink some more water.

11. O.K. Good. It went down.

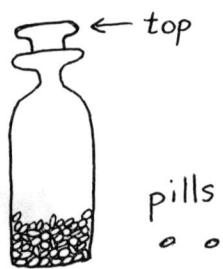

SHARPENING YOUR PENCIL

1. Pick up your pencil.

2. Look at the point.

3. Feel it with your thumb. It's dull.

4. Want to borrow my pencil sharpener?

5. Stick the pencil in the hole.

6. Sharpen the pencil.

7. Feel the point again. Ouch! It's sharp.

8. Clean the pencil sharpener.

9. Give it back to me.

10. Write ~~a letter~~ *your name*.

pencil sharpener

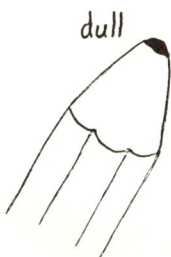
dull

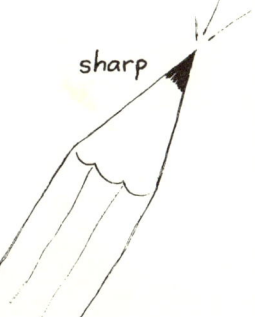
sharp

BREAKFAST CEREAL

1. You're going to eat some cereal for breakfast.

2. Open the box.

3. Pour some cereal in your bowl.

4. Spill some of it on your plate.

5. Pick it up and put it in the bowl.

6. Close the cereal box.

7. Sprinkle some sugar over the cereal.

8. Pour on some milk.

9. Take a bite.

10. Chew it up.

11. Swallow it.

SHOPPING FOR A COAT

1. You're going to go shopping for a new coat.

2. Look in the store windows.

3. Oh! There's a nice coat! Go inside.

4. Take a coat off the rack.

5. Take it off the hanger.

6. Try it on.

7. Look at yourself in the mirror.

8. It's too big. Take it off.

9. Put it back on the hanger.

10. Hang it up.

11. Try on another one.

12. This one fits.

13. Look at the price tag.

14. How much is it?

15. Buy it.

A GLASS OF MILK

1. Pour yourself a glass of milk.

2. Spill some of it on the table.
    Woops!

3. Go to the sink.

4. Pick up a rag.

5. Get it wet.

6. Wring it out.

7. Go back and wipe up the milk.

8. Go back to the sink.

9. Rinse out the rag.

10. Hang it on the faucet.

11. Go back to the table where the milk is.

12. Drink your milk.

13. Be careful. Don't spill any more.

WRAPPING A PRESENT

1. You're going to wrap a present for a friend.

2. Wrap _____ in some tissue paper.

3. Put it in a box.

4. Put the box on some wrapping paper.

5. Wrap it up.

6. Fold the ends.

7. Take two pieces of tape.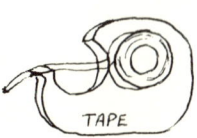

8. Tape the ends of the package.

9. Cut a piece of ribbon.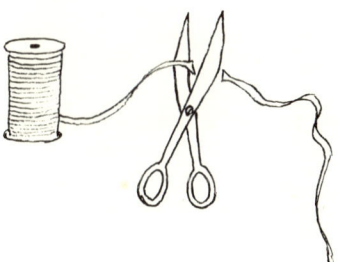

10. Wrap it around the package.

11. Tie a knot.

12. Make a bow.

13. Give it to your friend.

                  "Thank you!"

GOOD MORNING

1. It's seven o'clock in the morning.

2. Wake up.

3. Stretch and yawn and rub your eyes.

4. Get up.

5. Do your exercises.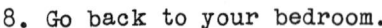

6. Go to the bathroom.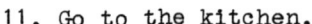

7. Wash your face.

8. Go back to your bedroom.

9. Get dressed.

10. Make the bed.

11. Go to the kitchen.

12. Eat breakfast.

13. Read the newspaper.

14. Go to the bathroom and brush your teeth.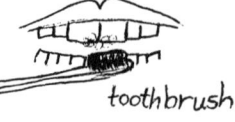
    toothbrush

15. Put on your coat.

16. Kiss your family goodbye.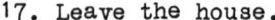

17. Leave the house.

YOU'RE GETTING SICK

1. You don't feel well.

2. Cover your nose and sneeze.

3. Take out your handkerchief.

4. Blow your nose.

5. Wipe your eyes.

6. Cover your mouth and cough.

7. Leave the house.

8. Go to the drugstore.

9. Oh, you're very weak! Fall down.

10. Get up.

11. Go into the drugstore.

12. Buy some aspirin, kleenex and eye drops.

13. Go home and take care of yourself.

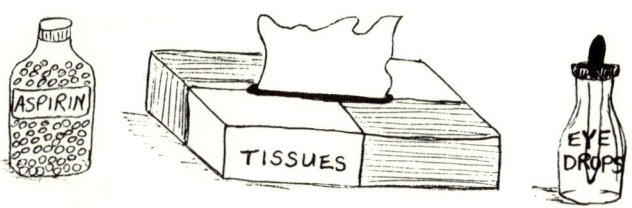

OFFICE WORKER

1. You're a man working in an office.

2. Sit at your desk.

3. Relax.

4. Loosen your tie.

5. Unbutton your jacket.

6. Take it off.

7. Roll up your sleeves.

8. Untie your shoes.

9. Uh-oh! Here comes the boss!

10. Tighten your tie.

11. Put on your jacket.

12. Button it up.

13. Tie your shoes.

14. Get to work.

15. Say hello to the boss.

SEWING ON A BUTTON

1. You're going to sew on a button.

2. Cut a piece of thread.

3. Thread the needle.

4. Tie a knot at the end.

5. Stick the needle through the cloth.

6. Put it through a hole in the button.

7. Put it through the other hole.

8. Stick it back through the cloth.

9. Pull it tight.

10. Do it again and again.

11. Finish it.

12. Bite the thread off.

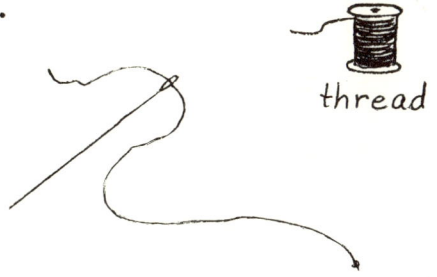
thread

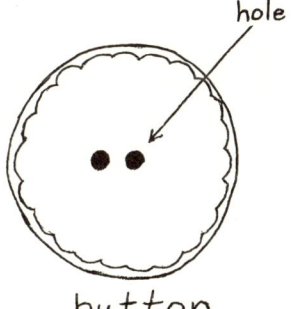
hole
button

PAINTING A PICTURE

1. You're going to paint a picture.

2. Spread out some old newspapers.

3. Take out a piece of paper.

4. Open the jar of yellow paint.

5. Pick up the paintbrush.

6. Dip it in the paint.

7. Paint a _____.

8. Let it dry.

9. Close the jar of paint and put it away.

10. Wash the paint out of the brush.

11. Wipe it dry on a rag.

12. Hang the painting on the wall.

13. Fold up the newspapers.

14. Put them away.

TAKING THE PLANE

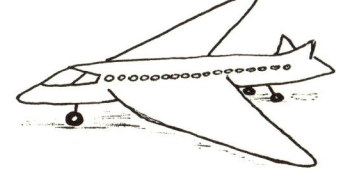

1. You're going to Hawaii.

2. Get on the plane.

3. Look for your seat number.

4. Sit down.

5. Fasten your seatbelt.

6. It's too tight.

7. Loosen it.

8. That's too loose.

9. Tighten it.

10. O.K. Here we go!

11. We're taking off.

12. Now we're flying through the air.

13. Unfasten your seatbelt.

14. Are you comfortable?   (Yes, I am.)

15. Enjoy your flight.

STOP! THIEF!

1. You're going to rob a woman.

2. You're going to steal her purse.

3. Take out your gun.

4. Point it at the victim.

5. Say, "Stick 'em up!"

6. Grab her purse.

7. Uh-oh! Here comes a policeman!

8. Run away!

9. Stop! Thief! Stop!

10. Drop your gun. Drop the purse.

11. Hold up your hands.

12. Say, "Don't shoot me!"

13. You see? Crime doesn't pay.

RESTAURANT

1. You're going out for dinner.

2. Walk into a restaurant.

3. Find a table that's not occupied.

4. Sit down.

5. Pick up the menu and look for something good.

6. Oh, here comes the waitress.
   waiter.

7. Order steak, rice and salad.

8. Unfold your napkin.

9. Put it in your lap.

10. Take a sip of water.

11. Here comes the food!

12. Enjoy your meal.

OPENING A PRESENT

1. You got a present from your friend!

2. Look it over.

3. Feel it.

4. Shake it and listen to it.

5. Guess what's inside.

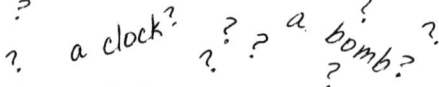

6. Tear off the paper.

7. Wad it up and throw it away.

8. Open the box just a little.

9. Peek inside.

10. Wow! It's just what you wanted!

11. Open the box and take it out.

12. Say, "Oh, thank you!"

A BALLOON TRICK

1. You're going to stick pins in a balloon without popping it.

2. Blow up the balloon halfway.

3. Tie the end.

4. Pick up a roll of scotch tape.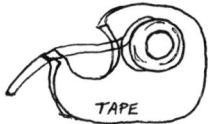

5. Pull out a short piece and tear it off.

6. Take two more pieces.

7. Stick them on the balloon.

8. Stick a pin through each spot that is taped.

9. Wow! It didn't pop!

10. Amazing! Fantastic! Incredible!

11. You're a real magician.

ICE CREAM AND T.V.

1. Go to the refrigerator.

2. Open the freezer.

3. Get the ice cream out.

4. Close the freezer and the refrigerator.

5. Put some ice cream in a bowl.

6. Leave the carton on the counter.

7. Go into the other room.

8. Turn on the T.V.

9. Sit down and watch your favorite program.

10. Eat your ice cream.

11. When you're finished, go back for more.

12. Oh no! The ice cream's melted! You forgot to put it away! What a mess!

TAKING CARE OF A BABY

1. You're going to take care of a baby.

2. Hold the baby on your lap.

3. Oh, what a cute baby!

4. Is that a girl or a boy?

5. Kiss her./him.

6. Hug him./her.

7. Squeeze her./him.

8. Offer him/her some cereal.

9. Feed her/him a lot.

10. Oh look! She's/He's spitting it out!

11. Ugh! What a mess!

12. Put him/her down and clean up the mess.

13. What a messy baby!

A BROKEN GLASS

CRASH!

1. Darn! You broke a glass.

2. Pick up the big pieces.

3. Be careful! Don't cut yourself!

4. Take them over to the garbage can.

5. Throw them away.

6. Go get the dustpan and the broom.

7. Go back to the place where you dropped the glass.

8. Lean over and sweep the small pieces into the dustpan.

9. Dump them into the garbage.

10. Put away the dustpan and the broom.

11. Go get another glass.

12. Careful now! Don't drop this one!

TO THE MOON AND BACK

1. Your hand is a rocket.

2. Your other hand is the moon.

3. Your lap is the Earth.

4. Take off.

5. Fly to the moon.

6. Fly around the moon.

7. Land on the moon.

8. Take off.

9. Fly back to Earth.

10. Try to land on Earth.

11. Uh-oh! Something's wrong!

12. The rocket is falling.

13. Crash in the desert.

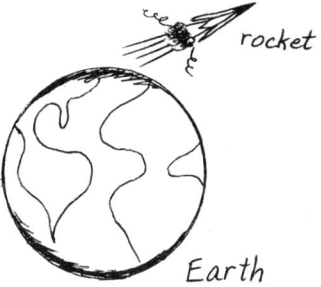

LET'S PLAY BALL

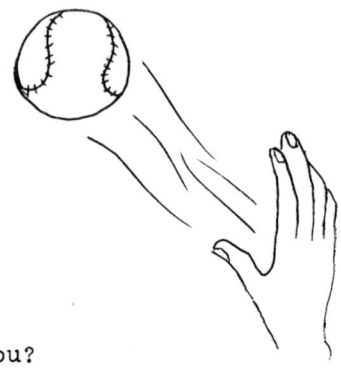

1. Hey! (John)! Catch!

2. Nice catch!

3. Throw the ball to me.

4. Oops! I dropped it.

5. Come over here and get it, will you?

6. O.K. Now bounce it on the floor.

7. Bounce it against the wall.

8. Try to catch it.

9. Aw! You missed it. Go get it.

10. Throw it up in the air.

11. Roll it to me.

12. Here you go! Good catch!

13. Now kick it to me.

14. Thanks. I've got to go home now. Bye.

15. Oh, by the way, want to play ball again tomorrow?

HUNGRY BUGS

1. Come to school.

2. Sit down.

3. Put your lunch on the table.

4. Uh-oh! Here comes an ant.

5. It's coming toward your lunch.

6. Kill it.

7. Wipe your hand on your pants.

8. Here comes a fly. He's on your lunch.

9. Kill him.

10. Uh-oh! Here come some more bugs.

11. Get them!

12. Quick! Eat your lunch!

USING A PAY PHONE

1. You're going to make a phone call.

2. Go into the phone booth.

3. Check the coin return........ Nothing!

4. Pick up the receiver.

5. Take out the correct change.

6. Stick it in the slot.

7. Listen for the dial tone....... Do you hear it?

8. Dial the number.

9. It's busy. Hang up.

10. Get your money back.

11. Wait a few minutes.

12. Whistle a tune.

13. Try again.

14. O.K. Good. It's ringing.

15. Talk to your friend.

SOUP FOR LUNCH

1. You're going to heat up some soup for lunch.

2. Pick up the can opener.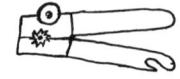

3. Open the can.

4. Pour the soup into a pan.

5. Add one can of water.

6. Stir it up.

7. Put it on the stove.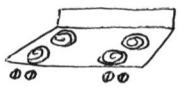

8. Cover it.

9. Turn on the stove.

10. Wait for the soup to heat up.

11. **Take off the lid and check it.**

12. It's ready. Turn off the heat.

13. Pour some soup into your bowl.

14. Take a sip.

15. It's too hot! Blow on it.

16. Wait for it to cool off.

17. O.K. Now try it again. Ah! Perfect!

CHANGING A LIGHT BULB

1. Turn on the light. It's burned out!

2. You have to change the light bulb.

3. Go get a new one.

4. Unplug the lamp.

5. Take off the lampshade.

6. Unscrew the old bulb.

7. Screw the new one into the socket.

8. Put the lampshade back on.

9. Plug in the lamp.

10. Turn it on. It works!

11. Throw the old bulb away.

BLOODY KNEE

1. You're walking down the street.
2. Fall down and skin your knee and scream.
3. Get up.
4. Cry. It hurts.
5. Look at your knee. It's bleeding!
6. Put your handkerchief on it.
7. Limp to the drugstore.
8. **Buy some iodine and bandaids.**
9. Limp home.
10. Wash the wound.
11. Put some iodine on it. Ow! It stings!
12. Blow on it.
13. Unwrap a bandaid.
14. Put it over the wound.
15. Throw away the wrapper.

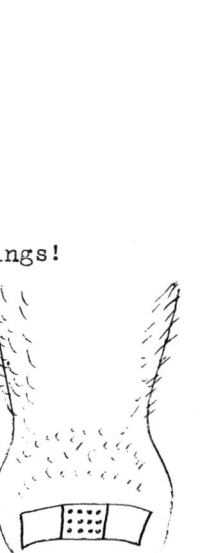

SCRAMBLED EGGS

1. You're going to fix scrambled eggs for breakfast.

2. Break three eggs and drop them into a bowl.

3. Pick up the egg beater.

4. Beat the eggs.

5. Add some salt and a little milk.

6. Mix it with a spoon.

7. Oil the pan.

8. Put it on the stove to heat it up.

9. Pour the egg mixture into the pan.

10. Cook it.

11. Keep stirring it.

12. When it's almost dry, turn off the heat.

13. Put it on a plate and eat it.

BANK

You will find a check on page 67.

1. You need to cash a check.

2. Walk into the bank.

3. Go over to a counter and write a check.

4. Sign it at the bottom.

5. Go get in line.

6. Wait in line.

7. Move up.

8. Walk up to the window.

9. Hand the check to the teller.

10. Say, "I want to cash this check."

11. Wait a couple of minutes.

12. Take the cash.

13. Count it.

14. Put it away.

15. Go out the door.

A BROKEN PLATE

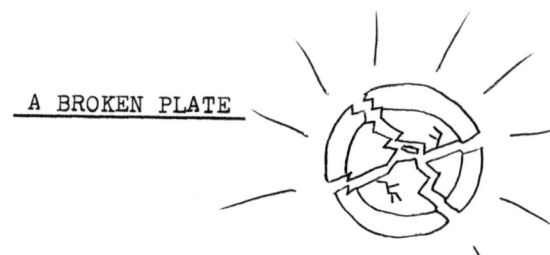

CRASH!

1. Uh-oh! You broke a plate. You better fix it.

2. Pick up all the pieces.

3. Put them down carefully.

4. Go get the glue.

5. Unscrew the top.

6. Squeeze the tube.

7. Put some glue on the broken edges.

8. Stick the pieces together.

9. Hold it tight for a few minutes.

10. Screw the top back on the glue.

11. Put the glue away.

12. Let the glued plate dry overnight.

13. Great! You fixed it!

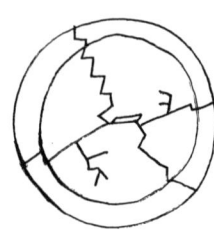

A MAGIC TRICK

1. You're going to do a magic trick.

2. Fill a glass with water.

3. Dip a piece of string in the water to get it wet.

4. Roll it in salt.

5. Put an ice cube in the glass of water.

6. Sprinkle salt on top of it.

7. Hold up one end of the string.

8. Lay the other end on the ice cube.

9. Wait a minute.

10. Say the magic word: "Abracadabra!"

11. Pull up the string.

12. Wow! Isn't that amazing?

13. You're a great magician!

WRITING A LETTER

1. You're going to write a letter to a friend.

2. Write the date in the upper right-hand corner.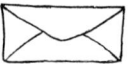

3. Write the letter.

4. Sign your name at the bottom.

5. Fold up the letter.

6. Put it in an envelope.

7. Lick the flap and seal the envelope.

8. Write your friend's name and address on the envelope.

9. Write your own name and address in the upper left-hand corner.

10. Tear off a stamp.

11. Lick it.

12. Stick it in the upper right-hand corner.

13. Take the letter to a mailbox.

14. Mail it.

GOING TO THE MOVIES

1. Go to the movie theater.

2. Buy a ticket.

3. Give it to the ticket-taker at the door.

4. Go into the lobby.

5. Buy some popcorn and something to drink.

6. Go into the theater.

7. Look for a good seat. **Here's one.** Sit down.

8. Watch the movie and smile.

9. Oh, this part is sad. Cry.

10. Wipe your eyes.

11. This part is scary. Open your eyes wide and scream.

12. This part is funny. Laugh.

13. Now the movie is over. Clap.

14. Get up and leave.

15. How did you like it?

MAKING A GROCERY LIST

1. Make a list of groceries that you need.

2. Don't forget butter.

3. Erase "sugar". You have enough sugar.

4. Cross out "candy". You don't need candy.

5. Underline "meat" so that you won't forget it.

6. Circle "bread". That's important.

7. Print "MILK" in big letters.

8. What a messy list.

9. Start over.

10. List only the things you really need.

11. That's better.

12. Cross out the first list.

13. Take your list to the grocery store.

14. Don't forget your money.

GROCERY SHOPPING

1. You're in the grocery store.

2. Go to the produce section.

3. Choose some fruit.

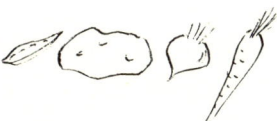

4. Put it in your cart.

5. Choose some vegetables.

6. Weigh them.

7. That's too much. Put some back.

8. Go to the dairy section.

9. Choose some eggs.

10. That's enough food. Go to the check-out counter.

11. Stand in line.

12. Say hello to the cashier.

13. Pay her/him for your groceries.

14. Wait for him/her to bag them.

15. Pick up your bag of groceries and go home.

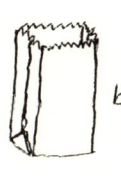

FIGHT

1. You're mad at your friend.

2. You want to fight with him./her.

3. Grab _____ away from her./him.

4. (He/She shouts: "Hey! Give that back!")

5. Hold on to it. Don't let go.

6. Push him./her.

7. Stick out your tongue at him./her.

8. Grab her/his arm and pull her/him.

9. Yell at her./him.

10. Punch him/her in the stomach.

11. Pinch his/her arm.

12. Squeeze her/his neck.

13. Let go.

14. Slap his/her face.

15. Kick her/him in the shins.

16. Scratch his/her face.

17. Hit her/him in the jaw and knock her/him out.

HAIRCUT

1. Your hair is getting long. You need a haircut.

2. Go to the barbershop.

3. The barber's busy.

4. Have a seat and wait your turn.

5. Read a magazine while you wait.

   "Next!"

6. Get up.

7. Go sit in the barber's chair.

8. Chat with the barber.

9. Watch him/her in the mirror while he/she works.

10. O.K. All done. Look at yourself in the mirror.

11. You look great! Get up.

12. Pay the barber.

13. What a terrific barber! Give her/him a tip.

EATING ORANGES

1. There are three ways to eat an orange.

    2. <u>Here's the first way</u>:

        3. Peel it.

        4. Pull it apart.

        5. Take out the seeds.

        6. Eat each section.

    7. <u>Here's the second way</u>:

        8. Cut it in half, then in quarters and then in eighths.

        9. Bite the pulp off the peel.

        10. Spit out the seeds.

    11. <u>Here's the third way</u>:

        12. Roll it between your hands.

        13. Cut a hole in one end.

        14. Squeeze the orange.

        15. Suck out the juice.

RAINY DAY

1. You're walking in the rain.

2. Stop. There's a big puddle.

3. Step over it.

4. Oh! It stopped raining.
   Close your umbrella.

5. Start running.

6. Be careful! There's some mud!

7. Slip in the mud.

8. Fall down.

9. Get up and look at yourself. You're all muddy!

10. Go back to the puddle.

11. Step in it.

12. Stamp your foot.   (Splash!)

13. Jump up and down.

14. Get out of that puddle!

15. Look at you! You're all wet!

16. Go home and change your clothes.

A ROUGH BUS RIDE

1. You're waiting for the bus.
2. Oh! Here it comes!
3. Get on.
4. Pay the driver.
5. Ask for a transfer.
6. Gosh! This driver is terrible! Fall down.
7. Get up.
8. Tell the driver to take it easy.
9. Sit down. Look out the window.
10. Bounce up and down.
11. Watch for your street.
12. There it is! Ring the bell.
13. Don't stand up until the bus stops.
14. O.K. **Now stand up and go to the back door.**
15. Step down.
16. Push the door open.
17. Get off the bus.
18. Wipe your forehead and say, "Whew! What a ride!"

BUILDING A FIRE

1. Brrr! It's cold! Let's build a fire.

2. Take your axe out to the woods.

3. Chop down an old tree.

4. Chop off a log.

5. Carry the log inside.

6. Set it down next to the fireplace.

7. Put some paper in your fireplace.

8. Put some small sticks on top of the paper.

9. Lay the log on top of the sticks.

10. Light a match.

11. Light the paper to start the fire.

12. Blow on it.

13. Fan it. Good! It's burning.

14. Sit in your rocking chair.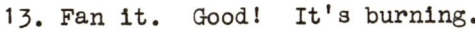

15. Rock back and forth.

16. Watch the fire. Beautiful! Fascinating!

17. Fall asleep in front of the fire.

GOING SWIMMING

1. You're going to go swimming.
2. Put on your swim suit.
3. Stand at the edge of the pool.
4. Hold your nose.
5. Take a deep breath.
6. Jump in.   (Splash!)
7. Swim across the pool.
8. Climb up the ladder and get out.
9. Go to the diving board.
10. Walk out over the water.
11. Dive into the water. Beautiful!
12. Swim underwater.
13. Hold your breath!
14. Swim to the surface.
15. Hold on to the edge.
16. Breathe hard.
17. Splash your friend.

A PIECE OF TOAST

1. You're going to eat a piece of toast.

2. Take out a slice of bread.

3. Put it in the toaster.

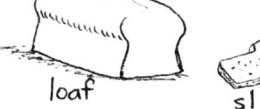

4. Push the <u>lever</u> down.

5. Wait a minute.

6. It's done!

7. Take out the toast and put it on your plate.

8. Spread some butter on it.

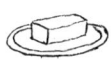

9. Watch it melt in.

10. Put a spoonful of jam on the toast.

11. Spread it around with a knife.

12. Cut the toast in half.

13. Pick up one half.

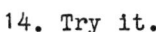

14. Try it.

15. Is it good?

16. Eat it all.

A BIRD

1. You're a bird in a tree.

2. Flap your wings.

3. Fly through the air.

4. Land on the ground.

5. Hop around.

6. Look for bugs.

7. You found one! Carry it in your beak.

8. Fly back to the tree.

9. Swallow the bug.

10. Sing to another bird.

11. Build a nest.

12. Sit in the nest.

13. Clean your feathers.

feather

14. Lay an egg.

nest

A BEAUTIFUL DAY

1. What a beautiful sunny day!

2. Sigh and go outside.

3. Stretch and yawn.

4. Lie down in the sun.

5. Oh, it's too hot!

6. You're sweating.

7. Sit up and look for a shady place.

8. Ah! There's a big shady tree.

9. Walk over to it.

10. Sit down in the shade.

11. Oh, it's nice and cool here.

12. Sigh and stretch and yawn again.

13. Lie down in the shade.

14. Go to sleep.

A PARTY!

1. You're having a party.

2. Put on some music.

3. Introduce two of your guests to each other.

4. Here comes another guest. Wave to her/him and shout "Hello!"

5. Offer some chips to some of your guests.

6. Eat some yourself.

7. Take a sip of your drink.

8. Clap your hands to the music.

9. Snap your fingers.

10. Tap your foot.

11. Nod your head.

12. Ask someone to dance with you.

13. Move your whole body to the music.

14. Face your partner.

15. Wink at him/her.

16. Are you having a good time?

17. Me too. This is a great party!

TIME TO CLEAN HOUSE

1. Boy, your house sure is dirty!

2. Put on your apron.

3. Sprinkle some kitchen cleanser in the sink.

4. Scrub the sink with a sponge.

5. Sweep the kitchen floor with a broom.

6. Fill a bucket with water.

7. Pour some liquid cleaner in it.

8. Stick the mop in it.

9. Mop the kitchen floor.

10. Dust the furniture with a dust cloth.

11. **Empty the wastebaskets.**

12. Plug in the vacuum cleaner.

13. Turn it on.

14. Vacuum the rugs and carpets.

15. Put all the cleaning stuff away.

16. Look around. It looks much better!

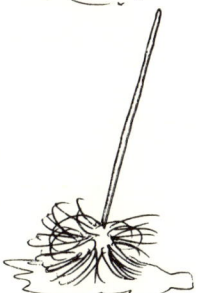

CAR RIDE

1. You're going to take a ride in your car.
2. Take out your car key.
3. Unlock the car door.
4. Open it.
5. Get in.
6. Start the engine.
7. Release the hand brake.
8. Put the car in first gear.
9. Drive away.
10. Change to second gear.
11. Speed up.
12. Shift into third.
13. Uh-oh! Too fast! Here comes a policeman.
14. Pull over to the side of the street and stop.
15. Roll down the window.
16. Say, "I'm sorry, officer."
17. Start to cry.
18. That did it! He's not going to give you a ticket-- this time.

DOG

1. You're a dog.

2. Here comes a cat!

3. Chase it!

4. It ran up a tree. Bark at it.

5. It's no use. Look for something else to do.

6. Sniff the ground.

7. There's an old bone! Chew on it.

8. Take it to the vegetable garden.

9. Dig a hole with your paws.

10. Bury the bone.

11. Here comes your master! Wag your tail!

12. Uh-oh! He's mad at you for digging a hole.

13. Hang your head. Aren't you ashamed?

14. Sit in the corner. What a naughty dog!

A MAN GETTING READY TO GO OUT

1. It's Saturday night and you're going to go out with your girlfriend.

2. Shave.

3. Cut your nails.

4. Take a shower.

5. Wash your hair.

6. Dry yourself.

7. Put on some cologne.

8. Get dressed.

9. Look at yourself in the mirror.

10. Comb your hair.

11. You look good.

12. Go borrow some money from your friend.

13. Buy some flowers.

14. Go pick up your girl.

15. **Have a good time!**

A WOMAN GETTING READY FOR A DATE

1. It's Saturday night and you're going to go out with your boyfriend.

2. File your nails.

3. Take a bubble bath.

4. Soak for a long time.

5. Shave your legs.

6. **Get out of the tub.**

7. Dry yourself.

8. Powder yourself.

9. Put on some perfume.

10. Get dressed.

11. Look at yourself in the mirror.

12. Fix your hair.

13. Put some fingernail polish on.

14. Put on your make-up.

15. You look beautiful! Wait for him to pick you up.

16. **Have a good time!**

AT THE LAUNDROMAT

1. You're going to do your laundry at a laundromat.

2. Sort out your clothes into two piles.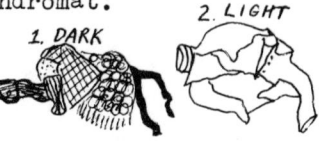

3. Put the dark ones in one machine and the light ones in another.

4. Add half a cup of detergent to each load.

5. Set the water temperature.

6. Put some coins in the slot of each machine.

7. Sit down and wait for the machines to finish.

8. When they're finished, take out your clothes.

9. Put them in a dryer.

10. Set it on medium heat.

11. Put some coins in the slot.

12. Wait for the dryer to finish.

13. When it's finished, take out your clothes.

14. Sort them.

15. Fold them up.

DOCTOR'S APPOINTMENT

1. You have a doctor's appointment.

2. Go to the doctor's office.

3. Tell the receptionist your name.

4. Tell him/her what time your appointment is.

5. Have a seat.

6. You're nervous. Sit on the edge of your chair.

7. Bite your fingernails.

8. Wait for half an hour.

9. Finally! Here comes the nurse.

10. Follow her/him into the examination room.

11. Say hello to the doctor.

12. Sit down.

13. Open your mouth wide.

14. Stick out your tongue and say, "Ah".

15. You're fine! Say goodbye to the doctor.

16. Ask the receptionist how much you have to pay.

PUTTING DROPS IN YOUR EYES

1. You're going to put drops in your eyes.

2. Open the bottle of eye drops.

3. Fill the dropper.

4. Put your head back.

5. Open your eyes wide.

6. Keep them open.

7. Hold one eye open with your fingers.

8. Squeeze a drop into it.

9. Don't blink!

10. Oh! You missed! The drop is running down your cheek.

11. Wipe it off.

12. Try again.

13. There! That's it. You did it.

14. Go ahead and blink now.

PUTTING UP A TOWEL RACK

1. You're going to put up a towel rack in the bathroom.

2. Hold the towel rack where you want to put it up.

3. Make four marks on the wall where the holes are.

4. Put the towel rack down.

5. Make four holes in the wall where the marks are.

6. Hold up the towel rack again.

7. Stick a screw in one hole.

8. Screw it in part way.

9. Screw the other screws in part way.

10. O.K. Now all the screws are in, but they're all loose.

11. Tighten them with a screwdriver. All the way in.

12. Great! They're all tight! Where are the towels?

CASHIER

1. You're a cashier.

                          You will find a check, a credit card and a driver's license on page 67.

2. A customer wants you to change a ten-dollar bill.

3. Take the ten.

4. Give her/him the change as you count it.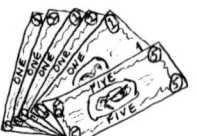

5. Another customer wants to cash a check.

6. Ask him/her for his/her I.D.:
   "May I see your driver's license and a credit card?"

7. Look at her/his driver's license.

8. On the back of the check, copy the license number and the date of birth.

9. Look at his/her credit card.

10. Write down the name of the company and the number of the credit card.

11. Count the cash as you give it to the customer.

TAKING PICTURES

1. You're going to take some pictures of your friends.

2. Load your camera.

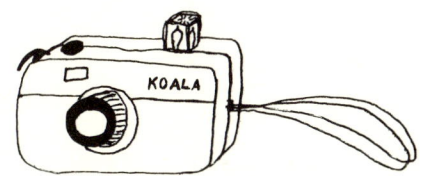

3. Wind it.

4. Use a flash.

5. Tell your friends where to stand:
   "Please stand over there."

6. Look through the camera.

7. Tell them to stand closer together:
   "Please stand closer together."

8. Tell them to spread out.

9. Tell (Peter) to sit down.

10. Tell (John) to move over.

11. Tell (Joan) to get in front of (Sarah).

12. Tell (Bill) to get behind (Tom).

13. Tell everybody to smile.

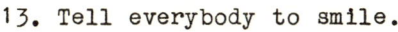

14. Press the button.

15. **Tell them all to stay where they are:**
    "Stay where you are."

16. Wind your camera.

17. Take another picture.

MAKING A TABLE

1. You're going to make a table.

2. Choose a nice board.

3. Take out your tape measure.

4. Measure the board.

5. Mark it where you want to cut it.

6. Pick up your saw.

7. Saw through the board.

8. Take out your hammer and four nails.

9. Hold a nail in one hand and your hammer in the other.

10. Pound the nail into the board.

11. Pound the other nails into the other corners.

12. Hey, that's a nice table!

13. Will you make one for me?

14. You're a great carpenter!

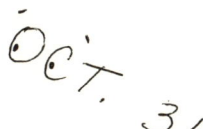

A JACK-O-LANTERN FOR HALLOWEEN

1. You're going to carve a pumpkin for Halloween.

2. Cut a circle in the top of the pumpkin.

3. Take it off.

4. Cut off the pulp.

5. Clean out the pumpkin with a big spoon.

6. Cut out two eyes.

7. Cut out a big scary grin.

8. Light a short candle.

9. Wait for the wax to melt.

10. Drip some wax in the bottom of the pumpkin.

11. Stick the candle in the melted wax.

12. Put the top on.

13. Put the jack-o-lantern in the window.

14. Clean up the mess.

A THANKSGIVING FEAST

1. You're going to have a Thanksgiving feast.

2. Set the table.

3. Take the roast turkey out of the oven.

4. Put all the food on the table.

5. Call your family to the table: "It's time to eat!"

6. Sit down.

7. Say grace.

8. Carve the turkey.

9. Serve some to each person.

10. Pass the rest of the food around the table.

11. Eat a lot.

12. Say, "I'm full."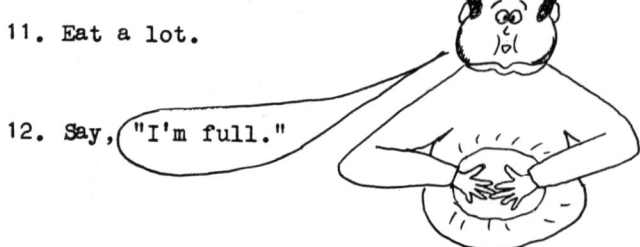

You have our permission to make copies of this page so that students can cut out the items for use with "Bank" (p. 35) and "Cashier" (p. 62). Or copy your own credit card, driver's license and check for this purpose.

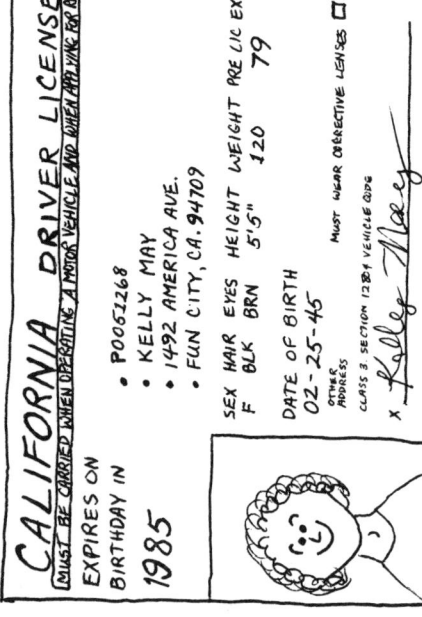

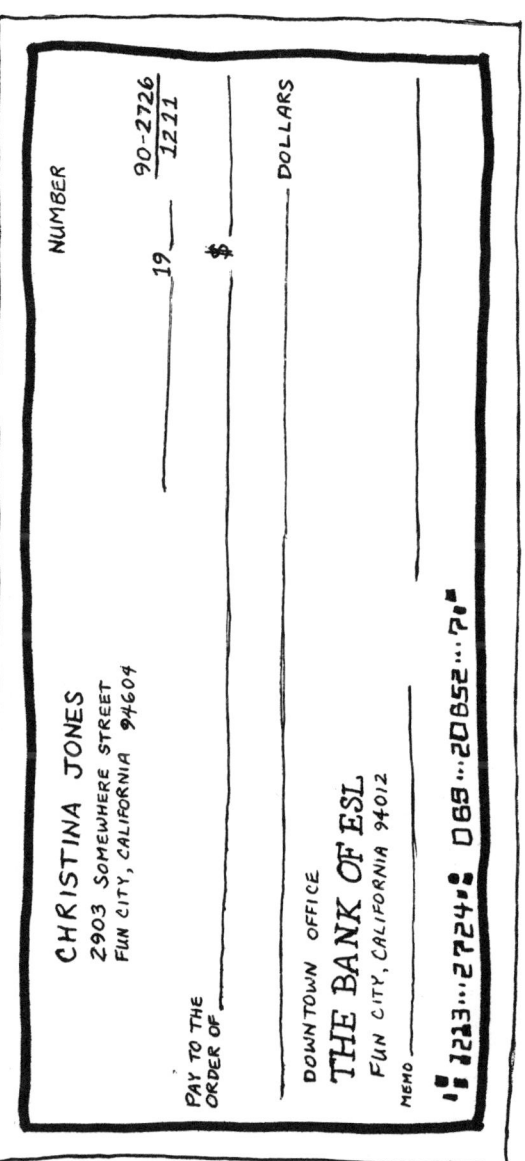

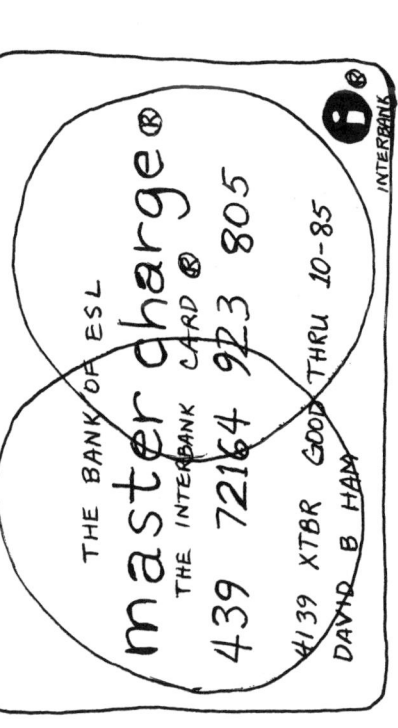

NOW CREATE YOUR OWN ACTION SERIES: *Making A Telephone Call*

1.

2.

3.

4.

5.

6.

7.

8.

9.

10.

11.

12.

ORDERING YOUR OWN BOOK

1. You want your own copy of this book.

2. It's easy! Turn to the next page.

3. Fill out the form at the bottom.

4. Cut out the form <u>OR</u> Copy it onto a piece of paper.

5. Write a check for the right amount.

6. Stick the check and the form in an envelope.

7. Address the envelope.

8. Put a stamp on it.

9. Go to a mailbox.

10. Mail your order.

11. Wait for your book to come in the mail.

12. When it comes, enjoy it!

    The first student text based on James Asher's Total Physical Response method. 66 action series -- each a lively one-page "happening" -- a list of sequential imperatives to be performed in the classroom with realia. Examples: Washing Your Hands, Going Swimming, Using a Pay Phone, A Magic Trick, A Car Ride (Take out your car key. Unlock the car door. Open it. Get in. Start the engine...etc.).

    Excellent for beginning and intermediate levels in high school, adult classes and college. Uniquely suited to multi-level and open-enrollment classes. Emphasizes survival vocabulary and can be used as the basis for a great variety of lessons, especially verb work. Includes general procedural instructions, whimsical illustrations on each page and a Foreword by James Asher.

To: The Alemany Press, 2501 Industrial Pkwy. W., Hayward, CA 94545

Please send me ____ copies of <u>LIVE ACTION ENGLISH</u> @ $5.95.
(California residents add 36¢ tax; for BART counties 39¢ tax).

Please send to: Name_____

Address_____

Price subject
to change   _____
without notice.   City   State   Zip